Talking about
Adoption

Jillian Powell

RSVP
**RAINTREE
STECK-VAUGHN
PUBLISHERS**
A Steck-Vaughn Company

Austin, Texas

Titles in the series

Talking about

Adoption • Alcohol • Bullying Death • Disability • Drugs Family Breakup • Our Environment

Published by Raintree Steck-Vaughn Publishers,
an imprint of Steck-Vaughn Company

Library of Congress Cataloging-in-Publication Data
Powell, Jillian.
Adoption / Jillian Powell.
    p.   cm.—(Talking about)
    Includes bibliographical references and index.
    Summary: Discusses adoption, the feelings of insecurity
    that such a situation may cause, and the nature of biological parents.
    ISBN 0-8172-5890-6
    1. Adoption—Juvenile literature.
    [1. Adoption.]
    I. Title. II. Series.
    HV875.P684   1999
    362.73'4—dc21   99-17811

Printed in Italy. Bound in the United States.
1 2 3 4 5 6 7 8 9 0 03 02 01 00 99

Picture acknowledgments

Cover (main) Martyn F. Chillmaid (background) Dennis Day

Eye Ubiquitous 6; Sally Greenhill 8; Topham 13; Tony Stone Image 24.
All other photography by Family Life Pictures/ Angela Hampton.

Contents

What is adoption?

Every one of us has birth parents,
a birth mother and a birth father.

Sometimes, our birth parents can't look after us when we are babies or as we grow up.

If this happens, we may be adopted by new parents. If you are adopted, you have adoptive parents as well as birth parents.

Why are some people adopted?

Sometimes our birth parents can't look after us because they are ill or they have died.

Some children are adopted from other countries because they have lost their birth families due to war.

Other children are adopted because their birth parents are too young to look after them. Sometimes, the mother is all by herself and can't cope alone.

Who is adopted?

Millions of people around the world are adopted. Children can be adopted when they're babies or when they're older.

You may not be able to tell whether or not a person is adopted.

You may have a brother, a sister, or a friend who is adopted, or perhaps you were adopted.

What does being adopted mean?

When you are adopted, you become part of a new family. Your adoptive parents will love you and take care of you.

Greg was adopted when he was a baby. His adoptive parents, Susan and Adam, love him very much.

Greg was adopted twelve years ago. He knows that Susan and Adam really wanted him because they adopted him.

Greg knows that they will always love him, and they will always be his adoptive parents. Adoption is forever.

Who are adoptive parents?

All kinds of people become adoptive parents, but they all want a child very much.

They may not be able to have babies of their own. Or they may already have children but want a bigger family.

Some children are adopted by a stepparent or by relatives such as grandparents or an aunt and uncle.

Isabel was adopted by her uncle Max because her own parents had died.

What happens when someone is adopted?

When people want to adopt a child they contact an adoption agency. A social worker from the agency then visits them at their home.

The social worker asks them lots of questions. They then try to find a child who would be happy with this family.

Kate and Pete want to adopt a child because they can't have any babies of their own.

They are lucky. The adoption agency has found a child for them to adopt. Kate and Pete are now looking forward to welcoming the adoptive child into their home.

What is a foster family?

Foster parents look after children when their birth parents can't take care of them properly. The children still belong to their birth parents, but they are cared for by a foster family for a while.

Later, they may go back to their birth parents, or they may be adopted.

When Gita's mother was ill, she was fostered by Ben and Milly. They looked after Gita for a few months until her mother was well again.

Who are foster parents?

Foster parents can be single people or couples. They may have no children of their own, or they may have a big family.

Sometimes, they have fostered lots of children at different times. All kinds of people become foster parents, but they all love and care for children.

What about your birth parents?

Some people are adopted when they are very young, so they can't remember their birth parents. Jane sometimes gets upset and would like to know more about her birth parents.

She finds talking about this with her adoptive parents helps. It took time to understand why she had been adopted and how much her adoptive parents loved her.

Can you meet your birth parents?

If you are adopted, you may know a lot about your birth parents already. You might have photographs and remember times when you were together.

Jack still writes to his birth father. His father sends Jack gifts, such as this book. They also meet each year on Jack's birthday.

Some children do not meet their birth parents until they are older. Robbie was eighteen when he decided to meet his birth mother. Now they meet every week.

But Robbie still thinks of his adoptive mother as his real mother.

What about your new family?

When you are adopted, you become part of a family. You may not look like your adoptive parents, but adoptive children often begin to be like their family in other ways.

24

When you are adopted, you may have other brothers or sisters by adoption. All of you will be part of the same family, and you will grow up together as a family.

Does being adopted make you different?

When you are adopted, you will become part of a whole new family. Your new life might be very different, but the most important thing is that you are loved.

Your new parents chose you. They will love you just as much as if you were their birth child.

Notes for parents and teachers

Read this book with children one-on-one or in groups. Ask them whether they can explain what adoption means. Ask them to think of as many reasons as they can why someone might be adopted.

Encourage each child to make a "life story" book. This can be a scrapbook or album and could include photographs, drawings, cards, train tickets, and written memories and descriptions.

The children could also write their own birth stories, such as where they were born, who their parents are, and what they know about them.

Adopted children may be sensitive on the issue of physical resemblance. Talk to the children about other ways in which we may take after our parents, such as the way we say or do things, the things we like doing, and the things that make us laugh. Point out that adoptive children can become so much like their adoptive parents that people often have no idea that they are adopted.

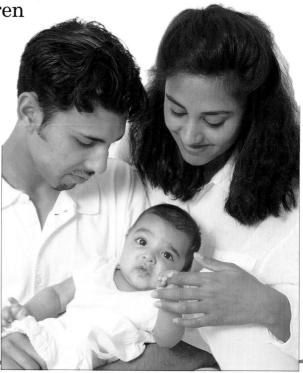

Talk about other kinds of adoption. The class or school could adopt an animal at a local nature park or zoo or a local building in need of funding. This project could provide the stimulus for drawing and writing from observation and for projects to raise funds.

Explain how some people decide to try to trace their birth parents with the help of adoption agencies. Talk about some of the issues this raises, such as how children and adoptive parents may feel and the fact that some birth parents may wish to be contacted, and others may not.

Ask the children whether they understand what fostering means. Ask them to think of some of the reasons that children may need to be fostered. Explain the difference between long-stay and short-stay fostering. Talk about the care provided by foster and children's homes.

Glossary

adoption agency A place where people go when they want to adopt a child.

adoptive parents Parents who have adopted a child.

birth parents The parents who gave birth to you.

foster parents Parents who look after a child for a while when their birth parents are not able to.

social worker Someone who helps families and elderly people especially if they are poor or in trouble.

Books to read

Cole, Joanna. *How I Was Adopted: Someone's Story*. New York: Morrow Junior Books, 1995.

Coran, Pierre. *My Family*. Minneapolis, MN: Carolrhoda Books, 1998.

Lifton, Betty Jean. *Tell Me a Real Adoption Story*. New York: Knopf Books for Young Readers, 1994.

McCutcheon, John. *Happy Adoption Day!* Boston, Little Brown, 1996.

McKay, Lawrence. *Journey Home*. New York: Lee and Low Books, 1998.

Miller, Kathryn. *Did My First Mother Love Me? A Story for an Adopted Child*. Buena Park, CA: Morning Glory Press, 1994.

Rogers, Fred. *Let's Talk About It: Adoption* (First Experiences). New York: Putnam Publishing Group, 1995.

Schwartz, Penny. *Carolyn's Story: A Book About an Adopted Girl*. Minneapolis, MN: Lerner Publications, 1996.

Index

Numbers in **bold** refer to pictures as well as text.